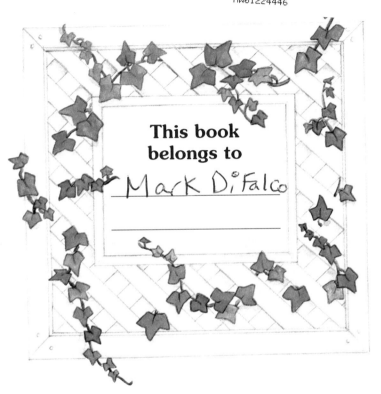

This book belongs to

Mark DiFalco

I'm VERY special to God!

When JESUS Was Little

Written by Sally Wilkins

Illustrated by
Mary Joseph Peterson, FSP

Pauline
BOOKS & MEDIA
BOSTON

Library of Congress Cataloging-in-Publication Data

Wilkins, Sally.
   When Jesus was little / written by Sally Wilkins ; illustrated by Mary Joseph Peterson.
         p.   cm.
   Summary: Recounts experiences that Jesus would have had as a child and relates them to similar situations in the life of today's young person.
      ISBN 0-8198-8293-3
   1. Jesus Christ—Childhood—Juvenile literature.   [1. Jesus Christ—Childhood.] I. Peterson, Mary Joseph, ill.   II. Title.
BT320.W55   1999
232.91'7—dc21

                              99–19065
                              CIP

Published in the U.S.A. by Pauline Books & Media, 50 Saint Pauls Avenue, Boston, MA 02130-3491.

Printed in U.S.A.

www. pauline.org

Pauline Books & Media is the publishing house of the Daughters of St. Paul, an international congregation of women religious serving the Church with the communications media.

3 4 5 6 7 8   10 09 08 07 06 05

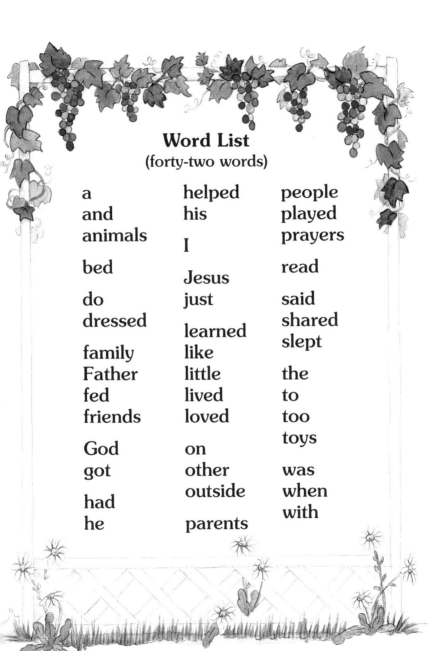

Word List
(forty-two words)

a
and
animals

bed

do
dressed

family
Father
fed
friends

God
got

had
he

helped
his

I

Jesus
just

learned
like
little
lived
loved

on
other
outside

parents

people
played
prayers

read

said
shared
slept

the
to
too
toys

was
when
with

For Parent/Child Sharing

Jesus is very special. Jesus is God's own Son. Jesus is God because God is his Father. Jesus is human, too, because Mary is his mother.

God sent Jesus to save us from our sins. This is why we call Jesus our Savior. God sent Jesus to earth as a little baby. Jesus had to grow up just like you. Jesus grew up in a family. Jesus and his family were Jewish. They loved, honored and obeyed God as the Jewish religion teaches.

When Jesus was little, he did many of the same things that you do. Can you guess what they are? This book will tell you about some.

Jesus had very special work to do. When Jesus grew up, he told us all about God his Father. Jesus told us that God loves us and wants us to be happy. Jesus died on the cross and came back to life again. Jesus did this so that we could all be happy and share God's life forever.

Jesus loves us very much! Jesus loves *you* very much!

When Jesus
was little
he lived with
his family.

Just like I do.

When Jesus was little
he loved and helped
his parents.

Just like I do.

When Jesus was little
he got dressed.

Just like I do.

When Jesus was little
he shared.

Just like I do.

When Jesus
was little
he played
with toys.

Just like I do.

When Jesus was little
he said his prayers.

Just like I do.

When Jesus
was little he fed
the animals.

Just like I do.

When Jesus was little
he learned to read.

Just like I do.

When Jesus was little
he had friends.

Just like I do.

When Jesus was little
he played outside.

Just like I do.

When Jesus was little
he slept on a bed.

Just like I do.

When Jesus was little he loved God his Father and other people.

I do, too!

BOOKS & MEDIA

The Daughters of St. Paul operate book and media centers at the following addresses. Visit, call or write the one nearest you today, or find us on the World Wide Web, www.pauline.org

CALIFORNIA
3908 Sepulveda Blvd, Culver City,
  CA 90230 310-397-8676

5945 Balboa Avenue, San Diego,
  CA 92111 858-565-9181

46 Geary Street, San Francisco,
  CA 94108 415-781-5180

FLORIDA
145 S.W. 107th Avenue, Miami,
  FL 33174 305-559-6715

HAWAII
1143 Bishop Street, Honolulu,
  HI 96813 866-521-2731
Neighbor Islands call: 866-521-2731

ILLINOIS
172 North Michigan Avenue,
  Chicago, IL 60601 312-346-4228

LOUISIANA
4403 Veterans Memorial Blvd, Metairie,
  LA 70006 504-887-7631

MASSACHUSETTS
885 Providence Hwy, Dedham,
  MA 02026 781-326-5385

MISSOURI
9804 Watson Road, St. Louis,
  MO 63126 314-965-3512

NEW JERSEY
561 U.S. Route 1, Wick Plaza,
  Edison, NJ 08817 732-572-1200

NEW YORK
150 East 52nd Street, New York,
  NY 10022 212-754-1110

OHIO
2105 Ontario Street, Cleveland,
  OH 44115 216-621-9427

PENNSYLVANIA
9171-A Roosevelt Blvd, Philadelphia,
  PA 19114 215-676-9494

SOUTH CAROLINA
243 King Street, Charleston,
  SC 29401 843-577-0175

TENNESSEE
4811 Poplar Avenue, Memphis,
  TN 38117 901-761-2987

TEXAS
114 Main Plaza, San Antonio,
  TX 78205 210-224-8101

VIRGINIA
1025 King Street, Alexandria,
  VA 22314 703-549-3806

CANADA
3022 Dufferin Street, Toronto,
  Ontario, Canada M6B 3T5
  416-781-9131

¡También somos su fuente para libros, videos y
música en español!